SHE'S JUST NOT THAT INTO YOU

THE FAB FEMME'S GUIDE TO
QUEER LOVE & DATING

ARYKA RANDALL

EDITOR-IN-CHIEF OF **TFF**MAG

"Relationships are a constant battle between acting from perception and responding to the reality of what you think it takes to love and be loved. Aryka's book offers insight that's open and straightforward. Truly a must read for any woman ready to hear the truth of what it takes to be in a loving relationship!"

— Chanel Brown, *The Real L Word*

"Aryka's voice and the advice she shares brings what some feel is taboo to the forefront. Love doesn't see race or orientation, it simply looks for passion and trust."

- Avian Watson, Sponsorship Director,
Publicist Traxx Girls Inc.

THIS BOOK IS DEDICATED TO MY GOOD FRIEND GABRIELLE WHO HAS NEVER GIVEN UP ON THE IDEA OF TRUE LOVE. KEEP FIGHTING FOR THE THINGS YOU KNOW TO BE TRUE IN YOUR HEART ♥

In memory of my puppy, MOLLY.
A girl's best friend through liFE, LOVE,
heartbreak & a whole lot of change.

-Molly

TABLE OF CONTENTS

iNTRODU(TiON

I hope this book finds you well. This keepsake was created in hopes of enlightening every girl who's ever felt like the "filler" girl who's only capable of finding people who are biding their time with casual dating until they can find "the one". You date for a while, maybe even meet a few of their friends and family members, and BAM! In the blink of an eye they tell you that they aren't ready to commit, or that they aren't sure they're ready to get serious... whatever that means. Fast forward a month or two after you stop dating, and the person is in a full-fledged relationship with some other girl they hardly even know. This, my friends, is the life of a "filler".

I'm here to tell you that there is hope for finding your true love regardless of how many times you've been some assholes' filler. Always remember that the beauty of love outside of emotion is the choice we make to allow a very special person to be a part of our world every day. Life is all about choices. The beauty in the freedom to choose, and the way we choose to do so is a reflection of our spirits. I hope this book reawakens your passion for love.

GROUND ZERO

IS LOVE FLEETING OR IS IT JUST YOU?

When was the last time you sat down and thought to yourself, "Why can't I conquer love? Is it me, or is love fleeting"? You're reading this book so it's probably safe to assume that this thought has run across your mind at least once or twice. While there are no definitive answers or theories pertaining to all things related to love, there are a few questions we can ask ourselves in order to cultivate happier, healthier relationships with the people we'd like to spend a few forever's with.

After every failed relationship, every heart break, and every heart to heart we have with ourselves and our friends, it's important to clear away the emotional fog and find some kind of resolution within ourselves. Every relationship is built to teach us something about who we are as spiritual beings. The more we resist the lesson in the outcome, the longer it takes us to get to the best version of ourselves, which, ironically enough, is who we need to be to attract who we want.

As women, we've been taught to move through life mindlessly squandering our time through messy relationships while searching for our soul mates (whatever that means). We're taught to be perfect and prim while waiting for "the one" to sweep us off of our feet and into an eternity of love and marriage. Masculine-identified people, however, have not been taught to live by those principals. At no point has society encouraged either party to go out and find themselves before entering into a union with another person. Herein lies the problem, and a very small part of the solution.

"BECAUSE I AM FEMALE, I AM EXPECTED _TO_ MAKE MY LIFE CHOICES ALWAYS KEEPING IN MIND THAT MARRIAGE _IS_ THE MOST IMPORTANT. NOW MARRIAGE CAN BE A SOURCE OF JOY & LOVE & MUTUAL SUPPORT, but WHY DO WE TEACH GIRLS _TO_ ASPIRE TO MARRIAGE AND WE DON'T TEACH BOYS THE SAME?"

— CHIMAMANDA NGOZI ADICHIE

It can be daunting to try to become the best version of yourself, but this process of self-discovery is essential in order to find your "true love". Here are a few key questions you should ask yourself in order to assess whether you are on the right track:

- How much time do I give myself to reconnect to my core being after a relationship?

- What are some things I can work on to bring more to the table mentally and physically?

- Am I capable of being happy with my daily activities without the companionship of another person?

- What truly makes me happy outside of relationships with friends, family, and loved ones?

Once you've answered those questions, go back to the first question at hand and reevaluate whether love is fleeting, or if it's just you.

One thing we can be certain of with all things pertaining to love is that there is a lesson to be learned from every relationship we partake in. Sometimes the lesson is large, sometimes the lesson is small. Either way, the lesson serves as an opportunity for us to learn more about who we are, and what we do/don't want in relationships. The longer we choose to ignore the lesson from each relationship, the more we stifle our chance at finding true love. Why? Because the universe will continue to present us with the same lesson over and over until we decide to take the hint. This is why we find ourselves dating towards the same outcome with different people. Our dating patterns are not a coincidence.

Something we should probably discuss before we go any further is the word love. What is love? More importantly, what is love to you? For many people, love is ego-driven. For them, love equates to an excuse to act rashly and make choices out of fear. It's an excuse to act cowardly or jealous. In reality, that isn't love because love and fear cannot exist in the same space. Love isn't measured on a scale of how much BS you put up with from someone. Love is selfless, not selfish.

To others, love is divine. It's freedom without fear. It's meeting someone who loves you unconditionally and trusting them as they contribute positively towards helping you become the best version of yourself. It's an action that takes place in the hearts and minds of two people who feel spiritually connected to one another. It has nothing to do with the fairytale that society has led us to believe for so many years.

If you're a person who loves from a place of fear, you probably find love to be fleeting. You analyze things and stay on the defense so you can protect your heart from the horror that is heartbreak. You try to control situations and people to avoid getting hurt. You're scared to death that the person you've decided to give your love to will shatter your world into a million pieces. While it's all quite dramatic and semi-entertaining, living in constant fear of being vulnerable is not a way to cultivate a healthy romantic relationship.

Now that we've had the "what is love" talk, we can move on to the next topic: expectations. The set of expectations society has trained young women to believe about love is completely unrealistic. We all have this image of what "the one" will be like embedded in our minds. Society says true love looks like a good Julia Roberts flick. The dating world says otherwise.

There's no lady-knight in shining armor that travels across a field on her snow white horse to rescue you from the woes of dating. You may not meet the love of your life in the Whole Foods produce department like you dreamed you would. Sometimes, you meet the person you love at a very unexpected time, in a very unexpected place. Other times, you may realize that the person you love has been a part of your life forever and you're finally seeing them the way you should have all along.

Don't expect for things to be perfect once you find "the one". We are human beings and we are perfectly flawed. We are emotional, we are passionate and we make mistakes. One impossible expectation we place on love is that it will be free from imperfections once it's obtained. There are still disagreements where there is love. There will be times when you get sick of each other and want to be left alone for the day, and there will be times when you just stare at her because she looks absolutely radiant and you can't believe she chose you. Both moments should be cherished equally, as they both help strengthen the bond in your relationship.

True love is never fleeting. The right relationship for you will always feel like it's within your reach. You won't have to beg for love or approval. You'll simply be required to be yourself and be open to love.

There's also a moment when you have to stop and realize that maybe the reason love is fleeting is because you're too fixated on the outcome instead of the journey. Maybe you're overlooking the woman who would be an asset to your life because she isn't quite where you'd like her to be yet. What if she's looking for you but she's too scared to reach out? Are you willing to be patient while she searches for the best version of herself? If not, then you don't deserve her love anyway.

If you wonder why love is so difficult for you to find, take a moment and look at yourself. Maybe the universe is trying to let you know that you have more work to do on your own before you can partake in a relationship with someone else. Happiness is a matter of perspective, so if you find yourself thinking "I'll be happy when I get into a relationship", you're already on the wrong path. Happiness starts from within and you can't offer someone else your love or joy until you've found your own. Don't rush through life searching for love. Let things happen organically.

Everyone has some kind of breakthrough or breakdown that leads to a journey of self. My moment of truth came after a five year relationship that ended via Facebook. Can you imagine what it's like to have a friend call you and inform you that your significant other changed their status to "single" for the world to see, and then blocked you so you wouldn't be mad?

When that relationship ended, I was numb. I mean completely numb. I didn't date anyone for almost two years after we split. While I was very lonely at times, the solitude gave me an opportunity to get to know myself better and fall in love with my talents and artistic capabilities. For the first time in my life, I learned to find happiness outside of a person. I learned to love life and cherish the time I was given to explore myself and the world. For me, this was ground zero.

PEP
TALK

IT'S NOT YOU, IT'S THEM.

Have you ever dated someone and thought things were
going well and then out of nowhere, they leave you high
and dry with some half ass excuse like "It's not you, it's
me"? Maybe not in those exact words, but you get the drift.
Sometimes when you meet someone and things end, it
really is them and not you. You can meet someone and have
the best intentions in the world for them but if they aren't
ready for the kind of love you have to offer, things will never
work. That has nothing to do with you.

The people you date are a reflection of yourself whether
you want to believe it or not. Every single person reflects

a different facet of your personality. Too often we ask ourselves, "How did I attract someone like this into my life? What did I do to deserve this drama"? Step outside of the box for a moment and think about things from a different perspective.

There's more than one reason why we attract the types of people into our lives that we do. One reason is that we present ourselves a certain way to certain people. We all have that friend who talks about wanting to build a home with Mrs. Right and settling down, but presents themselves like Ms. Bachelorette of the year to the public. That friend is probably the same friend who complains that the only girls who like them are the "thots". Well, here's a thought, you attract what you put out! You can't be in the club every weekend wishing for a wife. You have to embody the same characteristics and values that you would want in someone else in order to attain the person you desire.

Another way we attract the wrong people into our lives is by being mindless while dating. This usually looks something like the person who just got out of a long term relationship but can't stand to be alone so they date whoever, wherever, whenever to try and make themselves feel better. The random people you attract during this period are just as scattered and out of sync as most of the thoughts going through your head. No amount of frivolous dates and misplaced affection from a person you only know on a surface level will make you forget whoever broke your heart. Only time can do that.

People's perception of you sets boundaries on whether they feel that you're approachable or not. Be aware of the signals you send people through your dialogue and your body language. Again, become the person you want to attract. Don't be scared to be honest about who you are without giving it all away on the forefront. Don't let your ego speak louder than your truth.

Even with growth we can still find ourselves in relationships that aren't conducive to our health. Sometimes, it really is just them. Sometimes, the hardships we face while trying to love our other half have absolutely nothing to do with us. Sometimes, they do. The people who survive are the ones who learn how to cope with letting go of anything that's not "for them". Learning the difference between being in someone's presence because they want you there as opposed to "needing" you there is also imperative to staying away from people who probably aren't very good for you.

"NO MATTER HOW MUCH YOU LOVE SOMEONE, PEOPLE CAN ONLY TRULY MEET YOU AS FAR AS THEY'VE MET THEMSELVES. NO MORE, NO Less."

— ARYKA RANDALL

There are a number of categories people in the dating world fall into. Having the ability to identify people who aren't in your category will help alleviate some of the chaos from your life. You have the serial daters, who don't care who they date as long as their minds are preoccupied enough to divert their attention from the soul searching they need. You have the hopeless romantics, who long to be swept off of their feet and carried off into the sunset with their soul mate to get married and live happily ever after. You have the players, who date for no other reason than to occupy their free time and feed their ego, and you have the partygoers, who love the idea of love but love the idea of partying more. They generally settle into relationships with other partygoers, making it hard to maintain a relationship with one another in the real world where most people are sober throughout the day. That one usually ends pretty badly.

We could go on for days and days discussing the different categories that people fall into when dating, but what good what that do? Instead, let's focus on the bottom line: sometimes it's not us, it's them, and that's ok! The important thing to remember here is that identifying these people is only half the battle when it comes to dating. Identifying what it is you truly want and NEED in a relationship is the other half. The closer you get to yourself, the easier it is to weed out anyone who might pose a threat to your inner peace. The closer you get to yourself, the easier it is to figure out what you want and don't want in a relationship.

When things go south in a relationship, it's human nature to feel hurt and surprised and grieve the loss over a period of time. Let's get real though. Deep down inside, our gut feeling knows when things aren't right. We notice patterns, we observe, and we literally feel a shift in the energy between ourselves and our lover. The signs are always there whether we ignore them or not.

There are also signs that a person may not be on the same page as you in the early stages of dating. We want to see the good in people and we want to be hopeful that the possibility of real, true love is there. "Maybe this is it! Maybe she's the one." Or, maybe she's just not that into you and she's actually biding her time while you fall head over heels for the girl who cries wolf.

As women, we have to stop trying to fix people. We're natural nurturers and bringing toxic people into our lives to try and fix them has become a nasty habit. Not everyone wants to be fixed and some people stay true to who they are, regardless of how fucked up that is. You can't fix what's not broken and you can't make an apple into an orange. Learn the distinct difference between finding someone you can inspire to be a better person, and finding someone who's going to drain your energy while you try to fix all of their emotional problems.

If you're left wondering whether someone is ready for love, ask yourself these three questions:

- Does this person openly express the desire to be in a relationship?

- Have the two of you discussed goals and dreams for the future as sole entities and as a union?

- Do they speak on relationships and love in a way that seems inviting to you?

Avoiding red flags and continuing forward, simply so you can say you have someone, is never a good idea. Tread lightly and pay attention to what people show you, not what they say.

At this point, you're probably wondering how you're supposed to identify people who aren't ready for love. It's not as hard as it may seem, but it does take discipline and attentiveness. The first thing you can do is stop making excuses for people. No really, stop making excuses for people's non-compatibility with you. Use your intellect and ditch the emotion in the early stages of dating. Take time to really ask questions and have conversations that can shed some light on where things are headed in the future. If you know you want to travel the world with the one you love, child-free, then dating a woman with kids isn't a good idea. If you meet someone who is materialistic but you don't desire worldly things, then you may want to find someone who doesn't mind thrift store shopping with you. Do not make excuses for non-compatibility between you and potential love interests. You will only be hurting yourself in the long run.

Another way to avoid people who aren't ready for love is to present yourself in a way that makes it clear that you ARE someone who's ready for love. Sounds weird, right? Think about it like this. You wouldn't walk into a corporate meeting poorly dressed, with a half-finished presentation, and expect positive results from the CEO of the company. They have their shit together and you have to as well if you want to be taken seriously. When someone steps into your office, they need to have their emotional shit together right off the back. They need to be on the same page as you and it needs to be clear that you're in the market for love. That way they know how to present themselves to you.

One of the toughest parts of dating is learning to trust your gut intuition. Your gut will never steer you wrong when it comes to whether someone is right for you or not. A surface level connection with someone will always feel good at first, but it will weaken down the line. A spiritual connection will be strong and clear and unlike anything you have ever experienced before. There won't be a single doubt in your mind as to whether you should date that person or not.

We all have those friends who seem to date trash women even though they're a stellar catch. Yes, I said trash. Here's the thing about that topic. The only way to rid yourself or someone else of that habit is to be honest and able to accurately identify when someone is bringing toxicity into your dynamic. Internalizing things is complete BS! My friend Chanel literally created a list of things she will not tolerate in a relationship. Her strategy can be compared to drawing a line in the sand. If you cross the line, your ass is out. No mercy!

BACK TO BLACK

THE REALITY CHECK YOUR FRIENDS WON'T GIVE YOU.

As stated in the previous chapter, sometimes the problem isn't you, sometimes it's the other person. As lovely as that notion sounds, sometimes things do go south because of you. Has anyone ever pointed out your flaws before? When was the last time a friend or family member kindly pointed out your rough edges? Rough edges are beautiful, but we cannot accommodate them without first knowing what they are.

As human beings, we are flawed within our own right. Everyone's a little fucked up to some extent. The beauty in love is finding someone who cares enough to stick around while you learn more about yourself. There's absolutelynothing wrong with being flawed as long as you're aware of the things that challenge you.

At one point or another, we've all met someone who has ridiculous expectations for a potential love interest. They have to be a certain height and weight, drive a certain kind of car, have a certain kind of job, no kids, a clean driving record, blah blah, bullshit bullshit. The list of prerequisites to obtain a single date with this person is longer than the Constitution. The list goes on and on, managing to weed out anyone and everyone that may have the potential to make them happy. We all know at least one person like this. Rigid, unforgiving, and overzealous.

There are a lot of things your friends probably won't tell you about yourself that someone should mention. Being jealous, mean, too picky, not picky enough, clingy, etc. are all great ways to run someone off.

"I WAS DATING A GIRL WHO ONCE TOLD ME THAT I WAS DISMISSIVE & DIDN'T CARE ENOUGH ABOUT TRYING TO FIGURE PEOPLE OUT BEFORE SENDING THEM ON THEIR WAY. I NEVER THOUHT I WAS, BUT OVER TIME, I LEARNED THAT SHE WAS RIGHT & HEARING HER PERSPECTIVE WAS REFRESHING. IT WAS HONEST & IT CHANGED ME FOR THE BETTER."

— ARYKA RANDALL

Criticism is never easy to hear, especially when it's coming from people you love, but it's necessary to grow and evolve. Your friends will be in your corner while you embark on different dating adventures. Your real friends will check you about different things you do that may work against you in the long run. Allow their views to give you a fresh perspective on some of the things you may not see clearly.

After every relationship, there should be a period of time where you allow yourself to reflect on the events that took place while you two were together. Sit back and really think about what happened and, without placing blame on one another, pick things apart in a way that's healthy and inspires you to grow. What did you learn from that person and what did they learn from you? Did you push them away or are you happy with the way things turned out between the two of you? Was your breakup the product of some stereotypical lesbian miscommunication or was there love lost by way of disrespect or counterproductive activity?

Pushing people away is much easier than we'd like to believe. There are hundreds of reasons why people withdraw from romantic situations at the hands of the other person. Here are a few:

- People are clingy and get attached instead of loving freely by choice.

- People are mean. We're talking flat-out assholes. They aren't used to receiving love and they lash out at those who show they care because they're scared.

- People sabotage things before they can be the one to get hurt.

- People lack compassion and remain self-centered in a relationship.

- People's expectations of others are not the same set of expectations they place on themselves.

These are just some of the ways we tend to run people off while dating or in a relationship. Your representative can only hang around for so long before the real you comes out and rains on everyone's parade. Be aware of your flaws so you can become the best version of yourself and bring more to the table from a spiritual perspective. No one wants to date someone who can't acknowledge their flaws.

When you're single and you and your friends are playing the field, there's a good possibility that you will all become familiar with the women you each choose to date. Let's be clear about one thing. There is a huge difference between accepting your friend's criticisms about certain facets of your personality/relationship, and allowing them to criticize your relationship as a whole. Do not let everyone else's opinions of your love life or the person you are dating sway your feelings of happiness. Not everyone is going to love the person you decide to share your time with. Not everyone will approve of the dynamic of your relationship or the way the two of you choose to interact with one another. News flash! It isn't their life or their business, and as long as you are happy with the person you're dating, that's all that truly matters (unless the two of you are abusive to one another. Then your friends may have a valid point and you should probably ditch that psycho at all costs).

How much do the opinions of onlookers affect the way you feel about your relationships? The best relationships are the ones that other people don't always understand. They are the relationships where love and respect linger quietly. Love is humble and forgiving. Keep certain things to yourself.

IT'S NOT A

SECRET

IT'S JUST NOT

YOUR BUSINESS

The downside to telling friends and acquaintances your problems is the fact that it leaves a lot of room open for people to pass judgment and form opinions about things that don't pertain to them. If you and the person you're dating have issues and you run to your friends every time there is a problem, they will start to think poorly about the person you're dating. They will probably encourage you to stop dating them and find someone you won't always complain about. Can you blame them for feeling that way?

When was the last time a friend advised you to separate emotion from logic when dealing with a romantic situation? Once, twice, maybe never? Learning when and how to separate logic from emotion is probably one of the best things you can ever do for yourself. We're all guilty of overreacting from time to time, but some people take things way too far when it comes to letting their emotions control their surroundings. Separating emotion from logic and thinking in "black and white" is a perfect way to start weeding out people who don't belong in your life. It's also a good way to avoid dramatic situations that may leave you feeling uneasy or, even worse, in hand cuffs.

Here are few things to think about before going on an emotional rampage and doing or saying things you may regret later:

1. Count to ten. No seriously, count to ten. It works.

2. Speaking of the number ten, stop and think whether whatever is upsetting you will even matter in ten years from now. Ten, five, two, there's a great chance you literally won't give a single solitary shit about whatever is stressing you in the present.

3. Talk to someone older and wiser. Not a friend, but someone who's much older than you, much calmer, and has probably been in a number of relationships throughout their life. They may be able to give you a piece of advice you've never heard before that will help you in the long run.

4. Sleep on it. Sleep can cure just about anything. Boredom, the common cold, a bad attitude. ANYTHING! Don't be hesitant to sleep on any situation that's got your mind feeling off.

5. Step outside of yourself for a moment. Look at the situation from a friend's point of view. If your friend told you they were dealing with whatever situation you have going on, what would you tell them to do?

Do yourself a favor and learn how to think with intention. Your thoughts become things and they carry a vibration that literally has the power to shape your life and its circumstances. Be mindful, be brave, and be open to love.

Speaking of reality checks, I remember the last time I gave a friend a piece of advice about her love life. We're no longer friends. Not everyone can take the heat when someone tells them something honest about themselves. A true friend will always let you know when you're screwing up or when you're dealing with someone who may not be the best for you.

I also remember the first time one of my friends checked me about myself. It stung a little but it lit a fire under my ass AND helped me become a better person. I believe the words she used were "angry and mean". Why was I so angry and mean? Because I was internalizing my feelings instead of processing them.

BUILD HER AND SHE WILL COME

LOVE YOURSELF OR NO ONE ELSE WILL.

The most important part of a relationship is to tend to yourself first. A relationship becomes a 50/50 partnership only after you've become a full version of yourself. There comes a time in everyone's life when they have to stop and do some soul searching to figure out who they are. Before you can figure out who you are, you need to search for something bigger. Something spiritual that introduces a higher power into your life. Spirituality is the way to self-discovery. It's also the way to figuring out how to properly ask the universe for the woman you need in your life. Build her and she will come.

There are a few ways you can start to find spirituality within yourself. One way is by giving yourself more alone time. When you're with someone, there isn't much opportunity to really search yourself. There are distractions at every turn and you don't have time to focus on the things that are haunting you the most. With that being said, allow yourself some alone time to gather your thoughts, do a bit of reading, and get closer to yourself.

Another way you can start your journey towards self-work and spirituality is to do research. Read articles, collect books, talk to friends and family about their spiritual beliefs. Do all the research you can and figure out what resonates most with your morals and your heart. Take your time while searching.

"YOU NEED SOMETHING REAL IN ORDER FOR ANY OF THIS STUFF TO MATTER. YOU HAVE TO HAVE SOMETHING THAT'S FOREVER. SOMETHING THAT'S INVISIBIE."

- BEYONCE

The journey to spirituality will never end. We are constantly working on ourselves and our souls until we feel complete within ourselves. Even then, we may still find ourselves soul searching. The objective here is to do our best to become, you guessed it, a better version of ourselves. Sometimes, trying to attain this goal while entertaining a relationship can be nearly impossible, especially if it's with the wrong person.

Build her and she will come. What does that mean to you exactly? "Building her" has nothing to do with her per se. It's more about building yourself up to literally manifest the kind of woman you want in your life. When was the last time you sat down and really thought about all the qualities you are seeking in an ideal partner?

Realistic expectations of a partner and a relationship are needed to find the woman you want most. You can't have filet mignon expectations on a pork and beans budget. Learn to be ok with the reality of this present moment. You have to be realistic about the things you want and more importantly, the things you need. The girl with the fancy car, nice long hair, new bags and new shoes and fat ass may be nice to look at, but does she feed your soul? Does she want you to grow as a person, or is she all about herself? Does she respect your friends and family? Does she pray for you? These are the questions you need to ask yourself when deciding what kind of woman you're looking to attract, not whether she has a perfect physique or a perfect credit score.

Expectations vs. reality have the tendency to mess us up every time. Expectations of a fairytale relationship are why a lot of couples don't make it. Media has trained us to believe that love is a fairytale. Love is actually quite the opposite.

"LOVE IS A CHOICE. LOVE IS NOT A FEELING. PEOPLE HAVE MADE IT SEEM IN MOVIES THAT IT'S THIS FAIRYTALE. THAT'S NOT WHAT LOVE IS. YOU'RE NOT GONNA WANT TO LOVE YOUR GIRL SOMETIMES BUT YOU'RE GONNA CHOOSE TO LOVE HER. THAT'S SOMETHING IN LIFE THAT I HAD TO FIGURE OUT."

– JUSTIN BIEBER

Be realistic about your expectations for a woman and a relationship. Know that no matter how much you love her, there will be days she gets on your last damn nerve. That's life! The days she's hardest to love are the days she needs to be loved the most. The days you want to be selfish and tend to yourself are the days you need to give 50/50. Do not allow your expectations of a lover to cloud reality. True relationships are work and both parties understand that there is a process to building a healthy union with another person. Part of having realistic expectations of a relationship is to reprogram your mind to understand that things aren't always going to work out the way you want them to. You have to work towards understanding and continuous love in a relationship.

With expectations come a long list of things you need vs. things you want. What kind of woman do you NEED to help you grow into a better person? What qualities does someone need to possess in order to be an asset to your life instead of just dead weight? Again, the closer you are to yourself, the better you can assess what you need vs. what you want.

Generally speaking, the kind of woman that you need is going to be someone who pisses you off a little and makes you feel slightly uncomfortable. She will force you to grow in ways that hurt your ego and destroy your pride. In a sense, she's going to break you open so that new light can pour in, and change you into a better person. Growing pains hurt, so don't expect everything to be peachy keen all the time with "the one".

When you think about what you need from a girlfriend, think about the areas where you lack in life. Find someone who shares the same morals and values, but may be your opposite in other areas. If you aren't that great at meeting new people, date someone who's a social butterfly and can help pull you out of your shell. If you're someone who doesn't have the best spending habits, try dating someone who can balance you out by teaching you more about financial responsibility. The yin and the yang are the perfect example of why opposites attract and have an odd way of working out. It creates a balance in relationships. Everything in life is about love and balance.

Figuring out what you need from a partner also has to do with paying attention to the lessons that each previous relationship has taught you. When things don't work out with someone, there's always an opportunity to think about why and what made you want to leave the situation alone completely. What did you take away from the situation itself? What did you learn about yourself and what did you learn about what you do or don't want from a girlfriend? If you haven't already sat down and hashed out the gory details of your tangled past relationships, there's no time like the present! You absolutely have to address the lessons you've learned before you can move on.

Learning about what you need in a relationship is difficult because it requires you to revisit memories that aren't necessarily pleasant. Through all the torment and shame of exploring the trauma we've allowed others to inflict on our lives in the past, there is a clear understanding of what we need to maintain a happy, healthy relationship with someone in the future. It's important to analyze things so you can have a clearer understating of the present.

Visualization is a large part of attracting the kind of woman you want and need. Literally, visualizing the life you want will help fast track you to finding your ideal woman. Here's the thing. Your thoughts become things, so if you focus on the qualities you want in someone, you'll have a fair shot at attaining her. Sitting down and writing what you want from a partner is a good start, but visualizing a life with them is even better.

"A FRIEND OF MINE GAVE ME SOME GREAT LOVE ADVICE ONE DAY. SHE TOID ME TO CLOSE MY EYES & VISUALIZE THE WAY MY LIFE WOUID BE WITH THE GIRLFRIEND OF MY DREAMS. SHE TOID ME TO PICTURE OUR SHOES NEXT TO THE BED & TO IMAGINE US GOING ON TRIPS AND LIVING OUR LIVES TOGETHER. SHE TOID ME TO VISUALIZE EVERYTHING I WANTED & TO REALLY BEIIEVE IT WOUID HAPPEN ONE DAY. HER ADVICE WAS GREAT."

- ARYKA RANDALL

Visualization and meditation go hand in hand. One of the most amazing things we can do for ourselves is to learn to trust and believe that we do have some say over how our love lives play out. We aren't on auto pilot and there isn't some fairy godmother that's going to come and drop off "the one" at our front door. Dear lesbians, sorry to burst your bubble. Everything takes hard work, as well as the will to grow. There are certain steps that have to be taken in order to attract the woman of your dreams. Properly learning how to focus on that person will help you in the long run.

Have you ever sat down and drawn up a list of all the qualities you're seeking in a person? Over the years, as you've grown as a woman, have you revised that list to reflect the ways you've changed? After creating that list, did you strategically implement ways to find the kind of woman that will possess these qualities? When was the last time you visualized the things you were asking for? When was the last time you meditated and allowed the feelings of meeting "her" to fill you up and bring you joy?

Meditation and visualization both require a lot of feeling from the person practicing. You have to truly believe that the things you desire are going to happen and that they are already in motion to come into fruition. You have to focus and allow the things you're visualizing to fill you up. Smile, speak out loud, do whatever makes you feel amazing. Just make sure your focus stays on the qualities you want and need in a woman.

After you've focused on attracting your dream girl, it's time to put yourself in a situation where you can easily obtain her. Again, she's not going to materialize on your door step, so it's important that you put yourself out there to be discovered. Spending time in areas you genuinely enjoy is a good idea when you're looking to start dating. Explore places that feed your soul so that you can meet someone who shares the same interests as you. Take up any hobbies you enjoy and take trips to places that peak your curiosity. Open yourself and let the universe align you with the girl you need most.

Blind dates and hookups aren't always an ideal way to find love, but for some people, allowing a friend to pair you with someone they know will be compatible with you is a great way to go. Your friend is familiar with both of your personalities, your respective dating histories, and the kind of relationship you hope to share with someone in the future. For some, this technique is promising. For others, it's a complete disaster.

Physically putting yourself in a position to meet someone is just as important as mentally putting yourself in a position to meet someone. Believe it or not, people give off a certain energy that invites similar energy into their life. If you want to attract someone who is open to love, you have to be open to love. If you want to attract someone who's in it for the long run, you have to be in it for the long run, and so on. Projecting yourself in a way that's inconsistent with how you feel internally is a recipe for disaster. Be true to your desires and continue to focus on what you really want and need. Always remember to make yourself available mentally and physically.

One day, while sitting in my friends living room, tired and hung over, I had what I like to call a "kush epiphany". Slightly inebriated, I came to the conclusion that I was a serial monogamist. ME, can you believe it? Everything changed for me that day. I realized that instead of dealing with my emotions head on, I was transferring my same energy from one relationship to another, thus bringing the same experiences into every new dynamic.

After that day, I decided I couldn't continue dating people just so I wouldn't have to deal with baggage from my previous relationships. That was the day I decided to get myself together and stop perpetuating unhealthy dating habits.

PROCESS OF ELIMINATION

AVOID TOXIC RELATIONSHIPS.

What's the best way to avoid getting tangled up in toxic relationships before they occur? If anyone had a concrete answer to that question, there would be half as many episodes of Snapped on air. Everything is a learning process, but sometimes, we find ourselves in compromising situations simply because, well, we've made a stupid decision. For instance, let's say you meet a girl and you discover that she has the tendency to be violent early on. You get into an argument and she turns into a raging maniac and begins throwing random objects and hair at your head and breaking shit in the house. Don't ignore the red flags! If you spot signs of crazy in the early stages of dating, leave the situation alone and allow yourself time to figure out if that's really what you want to deal with in a relationship.

Another way to spot toxic people is to pay attention to how they treat other people. Do they have a lot of long-term friendships, or are the people in their life fleeting? Do they have siblings and if so, how do their siblings feel about them? Pay attention to the way they've left people after a breakup. Pay attention to the way they treat complete strangers and people who can do absolutely nothing to benefit them. If you're in a restaurant, pay attention to the way they speak to their waiter. People who aren't nice to their waiters aren't nice people, period.

People grow and change over time, so judging them based on their past isn't always the best way to go. However, there is absolutely nothing wrong with paying attention to their patterns. People's dating patterns say a lot about the way they choose to function in a relationship. Are they one of those lesbians who has a different girlfriend every month, claiming they're "the one" by way of social media? Are they the "player" type who can't seem to commit no matter how long they're dating someone? Do they have the pattern of dating one person until they find someone else who they think is an upgrade? These are all examples of toxic patterns you should watch out for in potential love interests. You can't force people to change into something they're not and you can't force people to live life to their fullest potential. People will only change when they're ready to. There's an episode of Sex and the City where Miranda compares men to cabs and women to passengers who are looking for a ride. The quote is pretty damn accurate as it pertains to masculine of center people.

"MEN ARE LIKE CABS. THEY CAN DRIVE AROUND FOR YEARS WITHOUT PICKING UP ANY PASSENGERS WHILE WOMEN ARE DRIVING AROUND WITH THEIR LIGHT ON BASICALLY SINCE BIRTH. ONE DAY THE MAN TURNS HIS LIGHT ON & PICKS UP THE NEXT WOMAN HE FINDS & BOOM! HE'S MARRIED. IT'S NOT STRATEGY, IT'S DUMB LUCK."

—SEX AND THE CITY

This quote also relates to people and the ways they do or don't change after long periods of time. Someone's decision to change has absolutely nothing to do with you and everything to do with them. Don't waste your time trying to turn a bopper into a housewife.

If you find yourself in a situation where you're unsure whether someone would bring toxicity to your life or not, ask yourself a few questions:

- Does this person have a toxic past?

- What is their motive for wanting to be a part of your life?

- What can you learn from this person?

- Are you both on the same page as far as having similar morals and values?

- Do they treat you well?

- Are they reckless with their emotions?

- Are they reckless with your emotions?

Do they make an effort to get to know you and learn your love language?

There are dozens of questions you can ask yourself to figure out whether you're dealing with someone who's toxic for you. The biggest challenge is to respond to these questions honestly and heed whatever answers you come up with. Don't make excuses to stay in a space that isn't good for you. If you aren't growing, you're dying, and toxic people will keep you down as long as they're in your life.

Sometimes, in relationships, people confuse healthy growth with toxicity. This is because growing pains hurt like hell and it's easier to slap a negative label on them and avoid them than to face the changes necessary to evolve into a better person. Realistically, anyone who doesn't help you create a space to change things about yourself isn't an asset in your life. Your partner should be someone who supports you and encourages you to grow and change and become a better person. Your true soul mate will take you on a journey of self-discovery that you didn't even know existed. The journey won't always be pleasant, but it will be worth it.

Accepting criticism from someone you love can be very tough. We want the people we adore to think highly of us and put us up on a pedestal to an extent. No one wants to hear the person they're romantically involved with say, "Hey you, you need to get your shit together." No one wants to admit that the representative they've been allowing to spearhead their relationship is finally taking a step back and that their rough edges are starting to show. No one likes taking responsibility for their baggage. No one likes having to revisit all the dark shit that's made them function the way they do in relationships. Opening old wounds hurts and no one in their right mind wants to do it.

THE WOUND IS the place WHERE THE LIGHT ENTERS YOU.

-RUMI

In your past relationships, have you dealt with someone who cared enough about you to say something if you were screwing up? Have you dealt with strong women or have you dealt with broken women who were unable to facilitate your growth? Those women cannot help you because they have not first begun to help themselves. Two broken people cannot repair one another, just like two happy people are less likely to suffocate each other with toxic behavior. You have to learn to love people who genuinely want to see you grow and are willing to take the time to grow with you.

To be clear, there are moments when you will date someone who isn't right for you and their criticism will be directed at you in a negative way because of their own internal issues. These people are toxic and are not making a genuine effort to help bring some light into your life. They just want to tell you negative things about yourself to make themselves feel better about their own shortcomings. Beware of these people. They are emotional vampires and they won't be ready to change until they grow tired of whatever is causing turmoil in their life. Misery loves company. Stay away from people who bring you down to make themselves feel more adequate. That's not love, it's mental abuse.

If you aren't sure what a toxic relationship looks or feels like, there are a number of ways to distinguish whether you're in one or not. The first way is by simply paying attention to how that person makes you feel. That doesn't mean that you should flee every time the two of you have an issue. It just means that if, overall, you find yourself unhappy with that person and the way they conduct themselves with you, it's time to consider letting go. A relationship shouldn't feel like a burden and no one should make you feel unappreciated or unhappy. Are you frowning most of the time or do you find yourself smiling when you think of your relationship?

Another way to spot toxicity in a relationship is to pay attention to the way the two of you communicate with one another. When you have a disagreement, is there growth afterwards or is it just another excuse to point fingers and place blame? How do you speak to each other when you communicate? Have they made an effort to understand the way that you prefer to be addressed in confrontational situations? Have the two of you mastered the art of actually having a conversation about your differences instead of screaming at one another?

One classic sign that you're in a toxic relationship is that you start to lose yourself. You lose sight of the things that make you happy, you become engulfed by your union, and you forget that you have an individual identity outside of your partner. A lot of women fall into becoming cheerleaders instead of team players when they enter a relationship. To have a healthy relationship, both of you have to be on the same team working towards the same goal. If one of you is sitting in the boat while the other person paddles frantically, guess what happens? The person paddling ends up going in circles instead of moving full speed ahead in the right direction. It's counterproductive and it creates negativity in a relationship. Do not be the girl or date the girl who allows their relationship to completely engulf their identity. Things become toxic when people lose themselves in another person. Mainly because they aren't filling themselves up with anything besides their relationship. This is a HUGE red flag.

The easiest way to tell if you're in a toxic relationship is that the relationship drains you. It literally takes all of your energy to maintain a relationship with your significant other and you still seem unsatisfied. Sometimes you will feel drained or helpless at the thought of loving her. You may even feel as if you're never capable of doing enough to keep your relationship afloat and healthy. This is one of the biggest telltale signs of a bad, toxic relationship. Don't ever allow yourself to be part of a relationship where you are not celebrated. Go where you are loved and appreciated.

What's a girl to do after leaving a toxic relationship to find peace and happiness? You throw a party and run the streets with your single friends! Not really, but in a sense you should celebrate yourself for being brave enough to leave before things got really ugly.

One thing you should try to avoid is letting a bad relationship change your views on love. Don't let a bad experience turn you into a hard, cold person who has their heart guarded like Fort Knox. Allow yourself to flourish and grow from the experience without becoming bitter. Avoid turning into the person who hurt you the most. Avoid developing a hard shell.

Another thing to avoid doing after ending a toxic relationship is distracting yourself from the pain of heartbreak. Avoiding the reality of your woes won't help you grow into a better person. As a matter of fact, avoiding your emotions will only result in a snowball of emotions that will hinder you from evolving as a lover and as a woman. Don't forget that you have to allow yourself to feel in order to learn the lessons you're meant to learn properly.

If you are a person who's become stronger after leaving a toxic situation, pay attention to the strengths you've acquired through heartbreak. Remember to be attentive without being paranoid when you decide to move on and explore things with someone new. Be picky about who you are guarded with and choose your battles wisely. Self-reparation is key to happily moving on without bringing old baggage into your future.

Avoiding toxic relationships didn't become easy for me until I took the time to learn what made me want to open my arms to people who weren't positive entities in my life. Learning to let go of people and things who weren't good for me was a hard lesson, but it was one I needed for my own personal growth.

Looking back on people I've dated in the past, I always knew when someone wasn't right for me. I just went along with things anyway out of boredom and desperation. When I first came out, I started dating a girl who treated me like complete crap. She would ignore me to entertain other women, lie to my face, and publicly embarrass me. She was the most toxic person I ever had the misfortune of coming into contact with. Lesson learned? Don't allow anyone to disrespect your energy or your heart. RID YOUR LIFE OF TOXINS!

THE U-HAUL AND THE FILLER

WHY SERIAL DATING LEADS TO DISASTER.

Let's talk about the filler and the U-Haul for a while. What exactly is a filler? A filler is a name for a person being used by a partner who's only biding their time with them temporarily while they search for "the one". In short, this person cannot be alone, so they date anyone who crosses their path simply to distract themselves from the idea of being single. These people go by the title of "serial monogamists," and their favorite person to date is, you guessed it, the filler.

Looking back on our love lives, we realize that we've all been a filler for someone at one point or another. Some of us were attentive enough to realize what was going on and some of us weren't. Every experience is a learning opportunity, so being a filler isn't completely horrible. If anything, it teaches you how to avoid people who are fighting a battle with themselves by way of other people. If you don't want to be a casualty of love, stay the hell away from anyone who's a serial monogamist. They will make you question the true meaning of love and suck your energy dry so they can fill themselves up.

This begs the question, are you a girl who uses fillers? When was the last time you dated someone for the hell of it? Or is there actually some kind of strategy implemented into your dating routine? When was the last time you were single and how long did it last?   Why did things end?

If you are a woman who uses fillers, there's a good chance you aren't even aware of your actions. Lesbians are almost never aware that they've become serial monogamists. Women in general aren't aware of their actions as it pertains to serial dating. Admitting you have a problem is the first step, so if you're having a hard time being honest about your reality as a filler, you're going to have an even harder time resolving the issues necessary to find someone you genuinely want to be with.

Lucky for you, if you are a girl who uses fillers, you'll be happy to know that there is hope for you to drop your unhealthy dating habits. First things first, you have to figure out whether you're a filler or not. Here are a few signs:

- You are always in a relationship.

- You get anxiety when you think about being single.

- Even when you're happy with someone, you're worried about who you'll date if the two of you happen to go separate ways.

- You go through the same motions in every relationship.

- You don't harbor any emotions after a break up that stop you from moving on quickly.

- You always have a "Plan B" in your back pocket just in case Plan A doesn't work out.

- You aren't emotionally invested when dating from person to person.

🌷 You can't stand to be alone at any given time.

🌷 You justify jumping in and out of relationships by blaming the failing relationship on whoever you dated last.

🌷 You're either vulnerable with everyone or no one.

These are all signs of someone who may be dating people as fillers to bide their time.

Inquiring minds would like to know: if you aren't filling, are you unknowingly acting as a filler for someone else? Have you evaluated the relationship you are in and/or pursuing in order to ensure you are out of harm's way? And by harm we mean some crazy ass she-devil who can only be alone long enough to pop a squat and light a cig. In a world where everyone is seeking love, it's easy to become involved with people who don't have pure intentions for you.

Being a filler is probably one of the worst feelings in the word. It makes you feel like you're underqualified to receive the kind of love you need and deserve. The person using you will never be able to satisfy your spirit completely and in turn, you will give your energy and emotions away without receiving any love back. A game of cat and mouse ensues and next thing you know, you're doubting yourself and wondering what you're doing wrong in your relationship. The key here is understanding that you will never ever be able to satisfy someone who isn't completely satisfied with themselves.

If you aren't sure whether you are a filler or not, there are a few steps you can take towards figuring out where you stand with the person you're dating. The first step is to have an honest conversation with them about where you see things going or what their intention is while dating. Are they dating for sport or are they looking for something long term? What is their dating history like? Of course the past doesn't dictate the future but it will help clue you in on what you can accept from your love interest as far as dating patterns are concerned. Be attentive to the way they leave romantic relationships and even more attentive to the way they start them.

Another way you can identify whether you're a filler in a relationship or not is by honing in on the signals the person in question is sending you. If you're all about them and they're constantly finding excuse after excuse as to why you aren't their "type" or why they just aren't ready to be in a relationship, chances are you are a filler. Women are notorious for trying to "fix" people or become the one that changes their mind about wanting to be in a relationship. If someone overtly tells you that they aren't ready for anything serious or they just aren't that into you, don't waste your precious time trying to convince them otherwise. Find someone who is searching for the same ending you are, even if you're going about it differently.

Filling is a very toxic habit for more reasons than one. For starters, when someone indulges in the practice of filling, they miss out on an opportunity to figure out who they really are as a person.

"YOU DO NOT NEED TO BE LOVED. NOT AT THE COST OF YOURSELF. THE SINGLE RELATIONSHIP THAT IS TRULY CENTRAL & CRUCIAL IN A LIFE IS THE RELATIONSHIP TO THE SELF. OF ALL THE PEOPLE YOU WILL KNOW IN A LIFETIME, YOU ARE THE ONLY ONE YOU WILL NEVER LOSE."

- JO COURDERT

Having knowledge of self and being ok with listening to your own thoughts is one of the most important lessons you will ever learn in life. It's impossible to make someone happy if you haven't found a way to make your own reality fulfilling.

When you become a person who uses fillers, you start to lose bits and pieces of yourself in every relationship. Navigating your way through love becomes foggy and the outcome of every relationship you enter into will be the same. You never learn the lessons you're meant to take away from each relationship. Instead of dealing with your shit, you bury your emotions and continue to snowball towards a reality of misery, disappointment, and loneliness. Avoiding yourself is one of the scariest activities you can ever partake in.

When you use people and relationships as a crutch to stall confronting your reality, nothing positive can come from your actions. Using people to bide your time with is indicative of two things: either you can't be alone, or you're hiding from yourself. Figure out which issue you have and take steps toward fixing it.

If you're a person who has a problem coping with solitude, there are a few things you can do to become more comfortable with the idea of being alone. The easiest first step to take is to spend a day by yourself. As weird as that may sound, spending the day alone will teach you a lot about yourself in a short amount of time. Go and do things that you enjoy. See the world, go to a bar and meet complete strangers and share details about your life with them. Open up and allow life's little treasures to fill you up. Get in touch with all the things that made you smile before life's mishaps stole your joy as an adult. Really pay attention to whatever makes your heart sing.

Another tactic that helps you learn to be alone is learning to quiet your thoughts. Much of why people dread the idea of being alone is because they don't want to deal with all the jumbled thoughts and realities running through their head. The solution to this problem is to learn how to think with intention. In order to create a positive, abundant life, you absolutely have to learn how to control your thoughts. Every thought in your brain carries a frequency as well as energy. When a large amount of energy is focused in one direction, realities are created and your thoughts begins to manifest. If you are in the habit of practicing thought with intention, you will be a much happier person and you'll lead a fruitful life.

Crying it out is also a great way to learn to be alone. No really, cry it out sometime! Allow yourself 48 hours to dig in the deepest, darkest corners of your heart and really peel back the layers of your past. Allow all the hurt and pain to consume you, but only for a moment. Stare your pain in the face, grab your heartache by the horns and say, "Fuck you heartbreak! I'm taking back my sanity." Cry it out, let go and release anything you are holding onto from the past.

When it comes to fillers, U-hauling and dating go hand in hand. Since most people who use fillers have an issue being alone, it's not uncommon to see them hurry up and move in with the young lady of their choice (for the time being). Beware of women who are eager to move in with you on a whim! Moving in together is a huge deal and while lesbians have mastered the art of U-hauling, no one ever said that it was healthy or productive. Let's talk about U-hauling for a moment, shall we?

Are you a U-hauler or a U-haulee? How do you feel about moving in with someone when you're still in the rose-colored lens phase? Are you a woman who is constantly scrambling to find a companion to move in with and share your space? Are you a woman who is comfortable allowing people into your space? If so, how long do you wait to get to know someone before you invite them to share a life with

"I REMEMBER THE FIRST TIME I U-HAULED. IT WAS THE LAST. HER KIDS DESTROYED THE HOUSE, SHE WAS ALWAYS LOSING HER BELONGINGS, & THERE WASN'T A WEEK THAT WENT BY WHERE ONE OF HER RELATIVES WASN'T ASLEEP ON THE COUCH IN THE LIVING ROOM. I FELT LIKE MY PEACE OF MIND WAS SNATCHED AWAY AT EVERY OPPORTUNITY. IF YOU CAN'T FEEL PEACE AT HOME, WHERE THE HELL ARE YOU SUPPOSED TO GO FOR ALONE TIME?"

— ARYKA RANDALL

you? All of these questions are pertinent to figuring out what kind of woman you are as it pertains to U-hauling.

U-hauling normally takes a very ugly turn once one or both parties realizes that things probably won't work out with their living arrangement. Little things may start to annoy you or you may discover that you simply don't like the person anymore after being around them all day every day. Sharing a home with someone requires more than love. It requires time, patience, and an understanding of what both of you need from each other to cohabitate in a way that's healthy for your relationship and your home life. Love has absolutely nothing to do with building a home together. It takes time to decide whether you should allow someone into your space to start a life with you. U-hauling should never be taken lightly.

Taking this one step at a time never hurt anyone, and realistically if you think the two of you will be together forever, what's the rush? After all, the journey itself is the adventure, not the destination. Don't rush to a finish line that's being held up by your insecurities.

You know what's scary? Being over the age of 30 and having absolutely no idea how to be happy without a lover. Serial daters scare the life out of me. Mainly because the ones I've seen navigate their way through life do it like a five year old kid at Disneyland. Slow and mindless. I didn't know what a true serial dater was until I met my friend Jane Doe. Obviously that isn't her real name, but we'll call her Jane to save face. Anyhow, my poor friend just can't figure out how to be alone. She bases her decisions around women and love and she enters new relationships before she's let the last one run its course.

Because she can't be alone, she always ends up with drama. She never has time to be by herself and figure out who she is or what she's passionate about in life. She pillages through the majority of the women in her path. Those same women come emotionally unglued once they figure out she has no idea what she wants. It's sad and dysfunctional. Nonetheless she's a great friend and I love her just the same... I'm just glad she isn't my girlfriend.

NO OTHER LOVE

IS HER LOVE WORTH THE BATTLE?

In most relationships, there is a runner and a chaser. The chaser is the one who is more spiritually evolved and adamant about expressing vulnerability. The runner loves the chaser but may not be as good with communicating their feelings to their lover. As a result, they are more apt to fleeing from situations that force them to communicate instead of working through them. This is how the runner/ chaser dynamic is created. In a situation like this, how do you know when a relationship is worth fighting for or when it's time to let it go?

If you're a chaser, then you probably aren't ever 100 percent certain that you should leave a situation. As a chaser, you may feel like it's your duty to keep things together because your other half isn't as skilled with articulating their feelings. You want to fix everything and fight for the relationship you love because it means the world to you and you've invested time into building it together. Things get hazy when you're constantly fighting for something that isn't meant to be yours. Pay attention to the signs.

How are you supposed to know whether a situation is worth fighting for or not? Are you making the decision to fight for your relationship just so you don't have to be alone, or do you genuinely want to be there? One of the worst things we as women can ever do is use all of our good energy to fight for someone who wasn't meant to be a long term part of our life in the first place. By the time we find a person we actually want to be with, we don't have any energy left to fight for a relationship that's actually worth fighting for. Herein lies the problem with hanging on to things that don't belong to us.

"*Let GO or BE DRAGGED*"

— ZEN PROVERB

A big part of being capable of exploring whether a relationship is worth saving or not is understanding how that relationship does or does not help you grow as a person. A healthy relationship always has a way of making you a little uncomfortable. Mainly because it's literally forcing you to grow spiritually. When you look back on the duration of time you've spent with whoever you are dating, what do you see? What have they taught you and what have you learned from every disagreement? If you haven't taken anything away from the relationship besides heartache and a bunch of mixed emotions, it may be time to let things go. If the two of you have grown and learned to accommodate both of your emotions by way of positive communication, then even with your differences, things are probably worth fighting for.

Women can be emotional at times and, as we discussed in the last chapter, there are a number of people in this world who hate the idea of being alone. When you have a problem being alone, you'll run into a lot of instances where you fight for the wrong people just for the sake of having someone. Not all love is good love, and if you're spending time in a bad relationship just so you can say you have someone at home, you're going to be emotionally drained by the time all is said and done. You're more likely to hang on to toxic people when you're grappling for something to hold on to.

When it comes to identifying whether a relationship is helping you grow or not, there are a few things you should keep in mind. The first thing is that you cannot grow if you aren't open to the idea of accepting tough love. You can't accuse someone of not having your best interest at heart when deep down you know that you wouldn't have openly accepted their advice away. Being open to criticism, tough love, casual observations, and a better knowledge of self are all required to be with someone who wants to help you grow as a person.

A wise man once said that arguments are healthy in a relationship and that some disagreements even make things more exciting. The chances that the wise man who uttered those words was drunk when he said them are 50/50 but either way, he does kind of have a point. Disagreements aren't unusual when you're dealing with two people merging their lives together. The problem comes when neither party is growing or learning from their miscommunications. Every misunderstanding is an opportunity to learn more about one another.

When you open your heart and mind to the idea of embracing change, you will start to see that you will navigate your way differently through every relationship you're in. You gain a clearer understanding of the ways that you've needed to improve to be the best girlfriend you can be. It also becomes easier to identify what point you made the changes necessary to become the best version of yourself.

Another thing you should ask yourself when deciding whether to put up a fight for your lady love or not is: what is it about her in particular that makes you want to stick around and sort out the bad shit from the good? Really sit and think hard about this question because the answer will help you save a lot of time if you're on the verge of moving forward with a toxic person.

Relationships and dating both require work. There will be important decisions that need to be made to ensure your happiness and theirs every step of the way. Choosing the right woman to build a future with is not an easy choice. People say when you know, you just know, but realistically, people think they know until they end up in divorce court. The only thing we really ever know is that we love that person enough to continue choosing them every day for the rest of our lives. Everything else is up for debate.

As cliché as it sounds, sometimes literally sitting down and hashing out a list of the reasons you want to be with that person versus the reasons you don't may be a damn good idea. Separating logic from emotion in a relationship is a skillset that not everyone has acquired. Being logical for a moment will accurately allow you to decide whether things are worth pursuing or not. Whoever you are with has to be someone you can grow with in the present and the future. Anything less is unhealthy.

When figuring out whether your lady love is worth the battle or not, make sure that there aren't any shallow factors fueling your decision to move forward. Good sex, fancy things, a big ass and supple breasts shouldn't have a single thing to do with your decision to keep someone in your life. Use your spirit and your intuition to make decisions about who to spend your days fighting for.

"I'LL BE THE FIRST TO ADMIT A FAT ASS CAUGHT MY ATTENTION. BUT NEVER MADE ME FAITHFUL. A PRETTY FACE GOT ME TO COMMIT BUT NEVER MADE ME CHANGE. IT WAS THAT FUNNY GIRL WITH THE BEAUTIFUL PERSONALITY WITH THE MILLION DOLLAR SMILE & A HEART OF GOLD THAT LEFT ME IN TEARS BEGGING FOR A SECOND CHANCE. I NEVER VIEWED WOMEN THE SAME AFTER HER. SHE LEFT MY HEART CONVINCED THAT LOVE WAS MORE ABOUT CHEMISTRY THAN BIOLOGY."

 — NAS

No truer words were ever spoken.

One of the cons to being in a relationship is that you will have to deal with disagreements. There isn't one couple in this world that's an exception to this rule. There are two kinds of arguments that take place in a relationship: healthy arguments and destructive arguments. Destructive arguments happen when two people are involved in toxicity that seeps over into their communicative norms. These arguments lead to a lot of screaming and name calling and back and forth drama that doesn't do either party any good. Destructive arguments involve taking below the belt digs at one another to make the other person feel bad about themselves. Nothing is learned, nothing is gained, and neither party walks away feeling they've learned anything from their discrepancies.

Healthy arguments consist of flared tempers that come from a place of love. Neither party is making personal attacks towards each other or hitting below the belt with their words. There is a hint of respect in every word exchanged even though the miscommunication is louder. Healthy arguments always lead to a better understanding of what you need from one another. Clarity and growth are the main outcomes of a healthy relationship. Which argument are you participating in? Being realistic about arguments is one of the best things you can ever do for yourself. Media has portrayed the art of love as some mindless event where two soul mates meet, fall in love and live happily ever after. We all know this is far from the truth, yet we still choose to pretend we're offended when things become challenging. Once the lust phase is over in a relationship, you can get down to real issues that matter and decide whether the two of you are compatible or not.

My mother used to say that you should always pick your battles in life. Whether they are with friends, family, or your children, you have to be smart about the battles you choose to engage in with people. Not every action is worth a reaction and not every disagreement will have a productive outcome. Don't argue about things that don't matter and won't affect you in the future. Every pointless argument you partake in will chip away the foundation the two of you are attempting to build together. Be careful about where you place your energy.

Quite the opposite of the fantasy world we've created in association with the word "love" is the harsh reality that plagues us all. You know the one: the reality that your relationship will never be perfect even with the perfect person. The best way to handle a very stark reality is to take something away from every disagreement you have. Use every opportunity to learn about one another's love languages and take time to learn what your trigger points are. Know that disagreements are there to strengthen your relationship, not destroy it. If your relationship takes a blow every time the two of you have a disagreement about something, you may be with the wrong person. Communication is key in any relationship.

Have you ever dated someone who made your entire relationship seem like some petty game of chess? Totally full of drama and constantly looking for something to be mad about? Ladies, when it comes to choosing your battles, steer clear of women who thrive on creating warfare in your life. Choosing to date a woman who thrives on drama is a battle within itself.

When you're deciding whether a relationship is worth fighting for or not, you should always assess whether you're fighting a battle or a war. Are the reasons for your discrepancies something serious, like infidelity or domestic violence? Or do your disagreements stem from something minor, like someone forgetting to make a phone call after leaving work? Understanding the kind of battle you're in for in your relationship will help you decide if it's something worth pursuing or not. Again, your time is valuable and you don't want to waste years of your life fighting for a relationship that was never right for you in the first place.

In every relationship I've ever been in, it feels like I'm the one who's fighting to keep things going. I'm normally the one who gets dumped and told I'm "too this" or I'm "too that". Most of the relationships I've been in weren't worth fighting for. I fought because it seemed like the "right" thing to do at the time. There was no real fire behind the passion in my fight for love. Maybe that's why things never worked out. It took me years to realize I was the only person in the ring and I was actually fighting myself.

READY, SET, LOVE

YOU'RE READY FOR LOVE, NOW WHAT?

When you meet the right person and decide you're ready to get serious about love, you'll need to take time out to make sure you're just as ready to be vulnerable as you are to be in love. Vulnerability is one of the most complicated emotions people deal with. Leaving yourself open to the possibility of being hurt or disappointed is scary as hell. Who in their right mind wants to open themselves up to someone and give them the power to shatter their whole little world in the blink of an eye?

Learning how to be vulnerable is all about having a strong sense of self. It's about knowing that you gave what you could and did whatever was necessary to create the best possible relationship. It's about advancing to a place where you don't require closure from the other party even if they let you down. Vulnerability is all about trusting yourself and your intuition.

How many relationships have you been in where you didn't allow yourself to be open and vulnerable? How did they turn out? Did you take anything away from those relationships or did they feel like a loss? If you've been navigating your way through love with a closed heart, chances are things aren't turning out too well for you.

"LOVE IS LIKE A BRICK.
YOU CAN BUILD A HOUSE,
OR YOU CAN SINK A DEAD BODY."

– LADY GAGA

There are a few interesting ways you can practice vulnerability without having to enter into a slew of romantic relationships. One thing you can do is make new friends and practice learning to trust new people. Whether you're dealing with friends or a lover, there is always some level of trust involved when people get to know one another.

Another way you can practice vulnerability is to have a raw conversation with someone you're already close with about your fears, hopes and dreams. Sounds silly, right? You'd be surprised how many women are completely fine with carrying on surface level relationships with people in their lives. True friends should be able to discuss anything from daily celebrity gossip, to where they see themselves in five years. Being open with the people in your life will help you become more comfortable being raw and unfiltered in the love department.

Making yourself inaccessible to anything related to love or vulnerability is a coward's move and usually the result of some heartbreak or disappointment that took place in the past. News flash, ladies! Your pain is not exclusive and anyone who's ever opened up to a lover has been gut punched at least once. We have all been dismantled by some asshole woman who ransacked our feelings and dragged our heart over coals. Do not allow negative past relationships to dictate the level of vulnerability you operate on. Do not allow someone else's dysfunction to ruin the way you feel about love. Always be hopeful when it comes to matters of the heart.

If you feel like you're not at a point in your life where you are ready to be vulnerable with a potential love interest, you may want to take some time and reevaluate your expectations of the word "love". No matter how much we think love should be stress-, drama-, and heartbreak-free, more often than not, we will encounter some kind of disappointment during the duration of a relationship. If your expectations of love are unrealistic, you may not have a clear understanding of why things take place that make you want to put up a wall.

Before you can be in a healthy relationship, you need to get your life together. Do all the things you wanted to do that require you to be a sole entity. Travel the world, have that threesome you always dreamed about, or take that yearlong internship in France your job offered you. Do all the things that you want to do before settling down. Let your inner hoe (yes, we all have an inner hoe, don't be bashful) roam free before you decide to commit to one lady, but be cautious! If your inner playgirl sticks around for too long, you may create a reputation for yourself that tarnishes your character when you are finally ready to be with someone.

A huge part of getting your shit together before partaking in a committed relationship involves making sure your finances are in order. People are reluctant to discuss their finances in the early dating stages of a relationship. 60 percent of the leading cause of divorce in the United States is because of financial differences between two parties in a marriage. One party may not have been honest about their financial standing before they decided to merge lives, or one person may have come into money or lost money somewhere along the duration of their relationship.

Another reason it's important to be financially stable before being in a relationship is because it's hard to enjoy exploring the world with someone else if both of you are ballin' on a budget. You don't need to be a millionaire but having the cash to hop a flight or take your lady love to a nice dinner on a whim will help keep the romance alive between you two. There's also a lot less stress involved between people in a relationship when money isn't constantly being brought up as a negative conversation piece. Having money woes in general is stressful; bringing someone else into the problem only creates a larger one.

Along with the issue of finances comes the topic of self-sufficiency. Make sure your living situation is conducive to a relationship before you just hop into something with someone else. Believe it or not, there are a lot of women out there who are looking to be taken care of or "helped" financially. Always make sure that you and your love interest both have a set living arrangement before taking on a relationship. You don't want to be one of those couples who winds up hating each other but can't leave the situation because neither of you can afford a lease on your own. Make sure you've got it before you try to give it to someone else.

Once you've decided you're in a place where you're ready to take things to the next level with someone, make sure you've made yourself available. Put yourself out there, be positive, and always keep an open mind when it comes to love. Remember to be open to the idea of love coming in a different package than you expected.

A few weeks ago, my friend Kenyatta and I had a conversation about when it's the "right time" for love. In a generation where people can have pretty much anything they want at the click of a button, how are we supposed to relate time to love without needing instant gratification for our efforts? Everyone wants someone who's already the best version of themselves but no one wants to be part of the work that comes beforehand.

Kenyatta and I agreed that when it comes to experiencing love, there is no right or wrong time. For us, it's all about living in the moment and choosing to love the person you're with every day regardless of how badly you want to punch them in the face sometimes. The right time for love is whenever it presents itself in your life organically.

TWIN FLAMES

WHAT TO EXPECT FROM "THE ONE".

After what seems like an eternity of work on yourself, you're all shiny and new and ready to open your heart to "the one". Do you have an image of what she will look like in your head, or did life rid you of false ideologues of what to expect from your soul mate? What about what you can expect from a twin flame? If you aren't already knowledgeable on the topic of twin flames, it's time to dig a little deeper to gain a clearer understanding of what finding "the one" really means.

"TWIN FLAMES ARE VERY RARE. TWIN FLAMES ARE TWO PEOPLE IN TWO SEPARATE BODIES THAT SHARE THE SAME SOUL. TWIN FLAMES MEET EACH OTHER IN THEIR FIRST INCARNATION SO THAT THEY REMEMBER THE SOUL FREQUENCY OF THE OTHER BEING. THEY ARE THEN USUALLY REUNITED ON THEIR LAST TIME TO THIS PLANET.

IF TWIN FLAMES MEET BEFORE THEY ARE READY, THEY CAN BE TOTAL OPPOSITES & NOT AT ALL COMPATIBLE. WHEN TWIN FLAMES MEET & ARE READY FOR EACH OTHER, IT IS THE MOST ENJOYABLE EXPERIENCE POSSIBLE ON EARTH."

— SOUL MATE RELATIONSHIPS

In short, your twin flame is a direct reflection of yourself. You share one soul and were cut from the same energy during the universe's creative process. When you meet your twin flame, it feels like you're coming home. It feels like you are reuniting with someone who has known you forever. The feeling is inexplicable and, quite frankly, one of the greatest feelings you can ever endure in your lifetime.

When you find a woman who is your twin flame, you can expect your relationship to be rocky initially. You'll notice that you and this person meet randomly and that the two of you may have quite a few obstacles to endure before being able to play a major part in one another's lives. You may be separated by distance or one of you may be in a long term relationship with someone else who is their soul mate. The major difference between a twin flame and a soul mate is that a soul mate can be found in just about anyone or anything. Friends, family, pets and loved ones can all come into your life in the form of a soul mate. There is no limit to the amount of soul mates you can have because each one is meant to teach you a different lesson. All of your soul mates collectively work together to help you evolve into the person you need to be for your twin flame.

Finding your twin flame can be overwhelming and confusing. Feelings arise quickly and there's a quiet intensity between the two of you that's undeniable. Everything seems perfect until it doesn't. When it comes to twin flames, feelings are more intense and senses are heightened. Everything is in limbo and time stands still for a moment. In one clear instance you figure out what's been missing from your life, or rather who.

Let's be clear about one thing as it pertains to twin flames. This relationship will require time, trust, commitment and an open heart to thrive. You will have to become the best version of yourself in order to attain a relationship that's so spiritually connected to the universe. This means twin flames only come together during their "last life" on this earth. A number of Buddhist teachings explore the idea of reincarnation and being reborn until you reach the highest level of nirvana. Those theories go hand in hand with the concept of twin flames.

As stated earlier in the chapter, finding your twin flame can be a scary and challenging experience. Most of the time, twin flames will meet before they are ready to embark on a relationship with one another. Experiencing such a strong energetic pull with someone while battling everyday differences can become confusing. The best way to get past these obstacles is to focus all of your energy on the bond you two share and less energy on the obstacles keeping you from being apart.

"IN COLLEGE, I HOOKED UP TWO OF MY FRIENDS WHO RANDOMLY RAN INTO EACH OTHER AT A TATTOO SHOP IN LAFAYETTE, LOUISIANA. THAT WAS EIGHT YEARS AGO. AFTER MANY FAILED RELATIONSHIPS, A MOVE TO CHICAGO, & DOZENS OF CONFRONTATIONS BETWEEN THE TWO, THEY MANAGED TO COME BACK TOGETHER, BUILD A FAMILY, & MAINTAIN A HEALTHY RELATIONSHIP. THEIR JOURNEY WAS LONG, BUT IN THE END, THEY'D BECOME THE BEST VERSIONS OF THEMSELVES WHILE THEY SPENT TIME APART.

NO AMOUNT OF DISTANCE OR TIME EVER REALLY SEPARATED THEM OR THE Love THEY HAD FOR ONE ANOTHER. THEY ARE PART OF THE REASON I STILL BELIEVE IN TRUE Love & TWIN FLAMES."

— ARYKA RANDALL

No one can take away what the universe has created for you, so regardless of how far the two of you may be from one another or how many disagreements you have while becoming one, you will always manage to find each other once again.

How do you identify a twin flame outside of the attraction you feel towards one another? Lez be honest ladies, lesbians have been wrong time and time again about who "the one" may be. A dozen roses, good sex and a few good morning texts later and, next thing you know, there's a U-haul parked outside of someone house. Be attentive ladies! Not everyone you vibe with is going to be the love of your life.

A number of published articles on twin flames state that there will be eerie coincidences that can shed light on who your twin flame is. Sometimes the two of you will look alike. No seriously, you two may resemble one another in many ways. Especially in the eyes, forehead, and mouth. Ironically enough, these are the parts of our bodies we use most to express our senses. You may notice that the two of you share a number of similarities surrounding your childhood or past experiences that helped shape you into the women you are today. In other words, your demons play well together.

Another sign that you've met your twin flame is that the two of you embody the yin and the yang naturally. Your strengths are her weaknesses and vice versa. Again, this can be confusing because society has convinced people that when you find "the one" everything will be serene. This isn't the case with the yin and the yang. Both are needed to maintain a healthy balance in a relationship. Having opposing views and opinions is okay as long as your values and core beliefs are similar.

There's a large chance that your twin flame will be a mirror of what you both fear and desire most in life. Let's elaborate a bit, shall we? If you're a person who is uptight and tightly wound, your twin flame will probably be someone who is social, carefree and a little naive. If you're a woman who likes to micromanage things and plan everything down to the T, you will probably find your twin flame in someone who lives life on a whim and enjoys random adventures. If you're creatively underdeveloped and/or repressed, you may end up with someone who appreciates the arts and can help open your mind to creative aspects of life you probably wouldn't have explored otherwise. Your twin flame will be the person who helps you become the best version of yourself. They will take you to another level spiritually and breathe new life into you, changing you forever. The two of you will want to rise as one to a place of euphoria and spirituality.

Understand that before you can be reunited (yes, reunited, because the two of you are already connected in a higher realm), you have to become the best version of yourself. There is no way around this! Even if you've found your twin flame, things will not flow harmoniously until you get in tune with yourself, your spirituality and the universe. In most twin flame dynamics, one person will be further along their spiritual journey than the other. One twin flame will serve as a muse or student, while the other takes on the role of a teacher. Being open to change and spirituality will help you on this journey. Read books, learn about yourself and become in tune with who you were destined to be this time around.

The reason both of you have to become the best versions of yourselves before you can live happily ever after is because that's what you both deserve. Your spirits cannot flourish in a dynamic where they are not appreciated. Growing pains and awareness of self are both required to reach your full potential.

Being prepared for your twin flame also means that you have to be open to becoming more spiritually enlightened.

If you're not ready to become more spiritual, then you aren't ready to meet the person you'll spend forever with. You have to be prepared to leave your ego behind and raise your thoughts to a higher frequency that will allow you to love that person freely and without doubt. This may require you to abandon some beliefs you've had about love or relationships in the past. Regardless of how challenging it is to release your ego, once you do, the two of you can come to a place where you move freely together, without ego or fear.

Because there is so much growth required for twin flames to truly come together, a lot of couples don't make it to the loving, successful relationship stage. The evolution required to maintain a relationship with your true twin flame is extremely hard to endure. There will be solid moments where you know everything is as it should be, and there will be moments where you want to flee and do what is easy as opposed to what is right.

Generally, when twin flames meet, there is a process that takes place where one woman becomes the runner and the other becomes the chaser. There may be a period where the two of you become separated and it seems as if your lady love will never return to the place you know she's destined to be. You can bet your bottom dollar that she's scared and resisting the changes necessary to build a healthy relationship with you. Hence the nickname "runner". When she runs, let her be free so she can take that spiritual journey and figure out who she is on her own.

The concept of twin flames can be a complicated one, but if you are dating with the intention of finding a lifelong partner, you may want to do some research on the topic to learn more on how to prepare yourself spiritually for Ms. Right. Get your shit together before she comes!

We've all thought someone was "the one" until they weren't. There's only one time I can recall thinking I'd met my twin flame. I'll never forget when I saw her. She stepped out from behind my friend's trunk with a HUGE grin on her face, khaki shorts, and a crisp white tshirt that was slightly wrinkled from the car ride. I felt a connection. A shift in energy if you will.

Getting to know her down the line, I realized that even when I touched the dustiest, darkest corners of her soul, I still loved her. I still believed her smile and our connection. Nothing has ever changed. She'll always have a piece of me with her. I'll always love her for unknowingly helping me learn what real love is about. To this day, I still believe she is my twin flame.

EL
FiN

IT'S NEVER REALLY OVER.

One of the most challenging parts of a relationship is that they are constantly changing. Growth doesn't stop just because you've found the person you're supposed to be with. The two of you will be on a permanent quest to learn about one another in a way that promotes growth and love. The learning process never ends because both of you are continuously evolving.

When it comes to love and relationships, it's important to understand that self-improvement will always be necessary in order to elevate the quality of your relationships. If you don't know who you are, how can you expect to offer anything to someone else? How can you work on a partnership with someone if you're incapable of working on yourself first? You have to learn to be okay with the fact that the work will never be over and that you will be need to learn about one another constantly.

Once you've found someone you really want to be with, it's important that you make definitive choices towards the future. Go about things with a plan so that there's direction in your relationship. Building together requires structure. The lines of communication between you two have to be open in order to ensure healthy conversation about the things you would like to build together.

The decision to love someone is a choice, as is the decision to be faithful, loyal, and happy. These are all choices that are consciously made by people committed to the idea of being in a healthy relationship. Again ladies, there's no lady-knight in shining armor that's going to come save you from yourself. All the saving has to be done on your own. Do not wait on another person or a relationship to bring you love. You have to create love from the inside out and then share the love you've created with someone else.

The purpose of this book is not to discourage you from your ideas of love, but to help awaken the lover in you who is searching for something real. Every one of us is looking for pure love. We all want someone we can trust who will be in our corner until the very end. All of these desires are within your grasp so long as you choose to keep believing in love. Remember that the one thing that transcends time and space is love. You are energy, you are the universe, you are divine, you are from love. Cheers to you finding your way back to love where you belong.

No matter how many books we read or how well we get to know ourselves, we will always be in a constant state of growth. As soon as we have things all figured out, something or someone will come along and challenge everything we thought we knew. Learning that nothing is ever really in our control is the best thing we can do for ourselves. Truthfully, it's the best thing I ever did for myself. Nothing is in our control, all we can control is the way we respond to things.

CONCLUSION

I'm sure you're wondering where I ended up after writing this book. Whether I took my own advice or not and discovered the love of my life with no hiccups along the way. Ha! As if. I'm still a work in progress. But I will say this: Within the last year, I have learned a tremendous amount about love, about life and about becoming the best version of myself.

As far as love goes, I still love the same person I mentioned in chapter 9. She's a royal pain in my ass but I wouldn't trade that pain for the world. During the duration of our relationship, I've learned to love without attachment. I've learned to be whole and vulnerable without expecting anything in return. I have begun to break out of the shell that was pain and step into love.

Writing this book was one of the most challenging and rewarding tasks I've ever completed in my life. I've never been good at managing my time, so being asked to complete a creative task on a deadline was foreign to me. The writing itself was a challenge as well because there were many times I realized the content was subliminally directed towards myself. Writing She's Just Not That Into You was therapy for me. It was a chance to address all of my own issues while helping other women address theirs. It was a chance to be brave.

I've been a writer for as long as I can remember. Storytelling is my gift to the world. The late Alan Rickman has a quote about the need for storytelling that absolutely hits home for me.

"And it's a human need to be told stories. The more we're governed by idiots and have no control over our destinies, the more we need to tell stories to each other about who we are, why we are, where we come from, and what might be possible."

-Alan Rickman

In the future, I plan on continuing to create relatable content that brings people all around the world together. At the end of the day, we are all connected by love. Without love, what is life? Thank you all for reading this book. May your lives be full of love, success, and great sex.

AUTHOR BIO

Aryka Randall is a 29-year-old writer and creative entity from San Diego, California who currently resides in Houston, Texas.

After moving to Lake Charles, Louisiana with her mother at the age of 18, she developed friendships with a number of people who would inspire her creatively later down the line. Around the age of 24, Aryka created a website called The Fab Femme with the intention of unifying femme women and men around the country, opening the door to a number of opportunities. She also created a web series called "Girl Play" that was highly successful online. The series itself was based on life after spending time on the gay scene in Houston.

An avid lover of Harry Potter, fashion, art, and pretty much anything from Tarte Cosmetics, Randall is your everyday femme with a Cali attitude and a southern spunk. Look out for more of her work in the future!

ACKNOWLEDGMENTS

This book is my first attempt to bring a little love back into the hearts and lives of anyone who's ever stopped in believing in the possibility of forever. Love is the one thing that connects us all. It's the one thing that transcends space and time.

I just want to thank everyone who has supported my dreams and goals over the years. I want to encourage you all to pursue whatever makes your heart sing. Live life in the present and understand that true love comes from within ourselves and pours into the people around us.

I want to thank all of my closest friends for encouraging me to keep love in my heart regardless of what I go through with other people. Thank you all for showing me unconditional love and pushing me to be a better woman.

I also want to thank Hugo and the team over at Mango Media for giving me a chance to be great and spread a little love in the world. You guys are awesome! Thank you for giving me the opportunity to shift humanity.

Lastly, I would like to thank my mother for always supporting my dreams and goals and introducing me to new concepts and ideas. I wouldn't be the rebellious, hopeless romantic I've come to be without her.